MENTORSHIP

THE PLAYBOOK

"For The Young Man as a Mentor or Mentee"

RAHKIM SABREE

TABLE OF CONTENTS

FOREWORD

Saint Peter had Jesus to mentor him for three and a half years. In those years Jesus protected Peter from Satan, warned him from himself, and then took time to teach him about how great he would be in the future. He knew that there was something great inside of Peter. Like all good mentors, Jesus knew he would have to be there to point out to Peter how great he was going to be because he knew Peter could not see or understand what it was that Satan wanted to take from him…

I had the honor of meeting Rahkim as a typical 14-year-old teenager searching for his purpose in life. He was always ahead of his peers, but behind in his life struggles. In truth, Rahkim took the struggles he encountered and allowed them to drive him to be the strong, positive, and focused young man he is today.

Rahkim called me every school day at 11:34 am for the first 3 of his high school years with a hunger to learn more about himself; something he wanted to learn from someone who would be both honest, and consistent. Two things I would learn he values greatly.

As his wrestling coach, I will never forget the time Rahkim learned the value of listening to the person coaching you to victory. The outcome of one particular match taught him not only a valuable lesson, but helped his teammates also understand the importance of trusting in the person you choose to guide you. After that match, the atmosphere in the practice room changed for the better.

When Rahkim shared with me that he was going to write a book on mentoring I was not surprised at all because I know this is his way of sharing an essential part of his life with others. In writing this book he will assist both mentors and mentees alike in understanding the value in helping others with words that come from his heart, a place I know he guards.

I am proud to still be watching Rahkim make his indentation in the world of mentorship from the shadows of mentors who have served as keepers of the flame. He no doubt has made it brighter.

-Wayne J. Woodbury

PREFACE

I wrote this book intending to share a piece of my mind, heart and soul with any and everyone who will receive it. It's highly intimate and highly introspective. It's *generally* for all of those who are unheard, broken, misunderstood, left out, hardened, ignored, unloved, under developed, or "normal" going through a rough time without the words to articulate what it is that they are experiencing. This book is specifically for the young man growing up, very often in the urban environment, who is no stranger to abandonment. Who has had to search for leadership, mentorship, and family outside of their own due to a lack of capacity and 'know how' in trying to figure out "how to be a man". There is no cookie cutter approach to addressing the needs of all young men but I'd like to think of this as a playbook. Please, take what resonates and part with what doesn't. My intent is to help by offering my perspective on the wants, needs, insecurities, and reflections that many may identify with. The contents herein are quite literally from the worn pages of my own journals over the years, and the many interpersonal relationships developed in that time. The stories I'll be sharing are stories that belong to me and the individuals involved in the experience. To protect their privacy, names have been changed and situations exaggerated or downplayed. The goal is to create a "call to action" to promote healing and understanding in others from the successes, failures, pains, joys, fears, frustrations, sacrifices, and enlightenment of my own experiences. I encourage all of you to be a mentor and to find a mentor. You never know what someone is going through or how their circumstances have shaped their growth and needs. Lastly, this book is for me…and only I will ever know what that means.

ACKNOWLEDGMENTS

This book is dedicated to my Grandfather, who has always been my biggest real life hero... Without his teachings I'd be one of the people I wrote this book for... Long live Baba and the Sabree Nation!
"A Luta Continua..."

This book is also dedicated to everyone who helped shape the completion of this book. From proof readers, cover creators, behind the scenes cheerleaders, constant encouragers and of course those who share in the experiences I'll be sharing in the pages of this book. It's dedicated to all the mentors out there who work tirelessly to make a difference starting with my own. Know that you've helped me as much as I've helped you.

Last but not least, this book is dedicated to Emily who told me that I NEED to write a book and share my story...

A COLLECTION OF LESSONS
AND EXPERIENCES...

COMPASSIONATE MENTORSHIP

It's generally accepted that the need for mentorship in young men is a void that can't be filled fast enough. I don't need to spell it out; fathers, grandfathers, uncles, brothers, and others are either missing from the scene, too busy, or too underdeveloped to really provide the mentorship needed because they themselves are seeking out the very same mentorship. They are often tired, busy, taxed, ill equipped, and inexperienced. However, what's probably not as well known and equally important, is the emphasis I'm placing on *compassionate* mentorship.

What does that mean, *compassionate* mentorship? That means that more than showing up and giving direction to a young man on how to tie a tie, or social etiquette, or how to change a tire, that there is a need for that young man to feel the intimacy of compassion from that mentor in knowing that no, this is not just an exercise to show you how it's done for the sake of showing you how it's done. It's the difference between TASK and PURPOSE. This is my acknowledging that as a mentor, YOUR mentor, that I am playing a very key role in either supplementing or filling a void that you need filling whether you realize it or not. This is my breaking down the stigma associated with men not having feelings, and discussing or expressing emotions. This is my committing to, and being conscious of your total state of being, (including your emotional disposition) and how to teach you to navigate that in a society that heavily taxes masculinity, especially in maturing young men.

I will not dictate how the mentorship role should look to people generous enough to fill them; however I will share from both the perspective of someone who once sought that role out to be filled, and someone who's filled that role for others. Young men are out there, looking for an acknowledgment of their total being more than we realize or acknowledge. Yes, they will make it difficult for you to get through to them, they will make you earn their trust to prove that you won't show up and then leave them high and dry. Young people today are too use to being let down. They will test you and do the opposite of what you tell them to at times, but they will enjoy the time spent learning new things and being taught the essentials of manhood. They will enjoy the time spent among men in an environment that allows them to be their authentic selves while acquiring the knowledge of what it means to be a leader, a mentor, a MAN. What is learned is just as significant as who is teaching it, and how they are made to feel while learning.

What I've observed, especially in minority communities, is that intimacy between young men is quite often expressed via rough housing (slap boxing/wrestling/etc), name calling or "the dozens", and other means used for the purposes of "toughening up" be it physically or mentally/emotionally. I find that this behavior is likely an adaptation for survival in an environment that attacks the young man's entire existence in his ascent to manhood and beyond. Intimacy is rarely expressed through positive verbal affirmations or non rough physical contact for fear of turning into a "sissy" or "punk". Male to male intimacy is masterfully tip toed around dancing on (or rather complete avoidance of) the lines of what is considered appropriate or "soft". It's quite clear however, that the need for intimacy coming from other men exists among young men. When expressed appropriately, that intimacy can foster growth, security, trust, brotherhood, and a lasting positive impact on the total being of the young man. When expressed inappropriately can stunt growth, create mistrust or resentment, feelings of abandonment or confusion, and a lasting damaging impact that not only ripples through the life of the individual, but all individuals he interacts with. My emphasis on the phrase compassionate mentorship is focused on incorporating those neglected behaviors, and redefining masculinity for the sake of emotionally healthy and mentally well rounded young men who will then repeat this with their children, siblings, nephews, friends, or future mentees, addressing a void that so desperately needs filling by minimizing the desire in young men to find that compassion through negative mediums.

Growing up, I was fortunate enough to have more than enough positive men in my life. Both my grandfather and my father were physically present my entire childhood and adolescence, and through them I was exposed to many men who demonstrated respect, and duty to the cultivation of a man-child into a man. I've never had to look to the streets for what the definition of a man was, and quite frankly even if I wasn't looking for the definition, my grandfather and father took every opportunity to articulate what a man is, how to be a man, and what a man's responsibility to himself, his home, and community was. Although now as an adult I can look back and understand that both they, and others took their responsibility and duty to raise me with guidance and structure seriously, my upbringing as far as I'm concerned, was very stringent and void of the compassion and an understanding of what I felt I wanted, needed, or observed from the relationship between other young men and their fathers by way of the very compassion I described above. Between the "yes sir's", the push ups, and the "be a man's" I believe an element of intimacy was missed that was later resented, and unconsciously sought out for in others who would provide it, something that could have ended poorly, corrupting everything my father and grandfather had worked for (and to avoid), simply as a result of someone else's willingness to understand me the way I wanted to be understood.

"I first started to understand the need for compassionate mentorship when I was about 12 years old. At that age it's important for a young man to feel trust and security in communicating with an older male. At that time, I was well into puberty and started to notice the change physically...clearly maturing in what seemed to me to be quicker than my peers and younger males. Although not quite an adult, it was a confusing stage because you notice things like hair under your arms when you're running around in short sleeves during the summer or new odors but don't see that in any of the other kids. I learned about the need for compassionate mentorship from a lack of compassionate mentorship. From the lack of (positive) acknowledgment of these changes. I was going to a summer camp several states away from my home, and one of the camp counselors was a black guy in a predominantly white camp. So we connected instantly on the basis of representation. He was the first adult male outside the sphere of my immediate family that demonstrated compassionate mentorship. Towards the end of the camp session it was quite clear that we'd bonded. He would drive me and my siblings home, buy us meals, we even had a video game night at his house. Towards the end of the summer we lost contact as I had returned home without reliable means of contact (this was before everyone had cell phones and long distance calls required a phone card). Although not intentional, I internalized that as a sort of abandonment, had hurt feelings, and learned to seek out that type of interaction time and time again into the future... The difference I think between him and say most other men who would role model in my life is that there wasn't a strict regiment or cadence to our interaction. It was unstructured, authentic, organic, and interactive. He didn't give orders but he acted with authority. He not only let me have fun but was part of the fun. That was the missing link I think."

The text within quotations came from a journal I kept. You'll notice throughout this text that this will occur many times over. I want to paint these scenarios for you using the same tone, same words, and same emotion I captured at the time of the writing. The camp counselor, we'll call him Calvin, was the first foreign mentor/role model I'd had. He had just graduated college, supported himself, accomplished athlete, and very positive not only with what he had to say but his intent behind it. He wasn't quite my parent's age but he was definitely older than I was. At the time I wanted to be just like him, "successful" in the eyes of society. Representation was everything. It was tough to grow attached to someone you look up to like that over a summer and have it abruptly end with feelings of abandonment. It was tough, but it created a need that I would later identify and deliver on for many others. And while they didn't all initially realize that need existed, they all benefited from it through consistency, through growth and self awareness, through compassion, even through the realization that life was worth living...

Sure, this appears to be a positive outcome to an uncomfortable circumstance. But that perception of abandonment also caused a fear of loss that followed me into every relationship to come, regardless of its nature. It caused an overcompensation to prevent that feeling of loss, and in some cases it caused me to compromise on standards and morals I had on friendship, religious discipline, destructive behaviors like underage drinking, frequent casual sex, etc. It made things like peer pressure harder to resist. It caused me to remain in relationships far beyond their expiration date. And while I'm sure in hindsight it wasn't Calvin's intention for me to be impacted or even perceive things the way I did, perception is reality in many instances...

If you are the mentee, this chapter should give you a canvas, or a clean page to begin to put the words together to start to express your needs to your mentor. You should know that your job isn't just to show up and listen. Your job is to get as much from your mentor as they are willing to offer you. If you are the mentor, this chapter should help start to expand your perspective around anticipating the needs of, and providing for your mentee. It should let you know you have a huge responsibility and some work to do. You are not a mind reader, but you were once a young man. Whether you had the needs filled by a positive mentor or a negative one, you know what that feels like, where that can lead you, and how that 'need' can be preyed on. It's my strong belief that your guidance is needed even if you have to fight tooth and nail to make your mentee understand, because one day they will understand, and they will thank you for letting your consistency beat their inconsistency. In the case of women mentoring young men, understanding society's programming of young men will be your key to "breaking through" but also by understanding that men model men, you can direct your mentoring efforts to include men to role model and relate to your mentee because like I mentioned with Calvin, "representation matters".

CALL TO ACTION #1

"Find a mentor, be a mentor!" If you are in a place to offer mentorship to someone younger or less experienced than you are, DO IT! It doesn't have to be complicated or formal; a cousin, a nephew, a younger brother, the neighbors kid, etc. Offer what knowledge or expertise you have, in your own way. At the same time if you identify someone as having a skill set or expertise that you don't and would like to have, or stand to benefit from having that individual's guidance and perspective, approach them and let them know you are building a mentorship network and you'd like to benefit from their mentorship. "Find a mentor, Be a mentor" is your first action item to deliver on.

Define what a mentorship relationship looks like to you.

- As a mentee do you want a particular mentor because you want to be associated with their name or personal brand?
- What, if anything, do you want to learn from them?
- Can your mentor be younger than you or close to your age?

- As a mentor is there some certain criteria you have before considering someone for a mentee?
- What if anything can you share or teach them?

CONSISTENCY

It's often discussed that at this time in society with the popularity that technology and social media brings (and the sometimes oversharing of our most intimate details and experiences) that we have a generation riddled with narcissism and outrageously unauthentic individuals. They do it all for "likes" and "follows"; the outfits, the experiences, the deeds, even the relationships. It's no longer about collecting a few true friends. No, it's more about having hundreds of social media friends and followers. Friends who know nothing about you but what you post or share or who you claim to be.

Social media has made it possible for people to simulate the social experience; never experiencing the trial and error of authentic friendships that stand the test of time and growth through the years. Furthermore, there are entire relationships built on the projections of social media posts, and people don't really know what it means to be or have a genuine friend. I ponder on whether or not the lack of experience in maneuvering an authentic social interaction, like friendship, can attribute to an increase in people who don't know how to manage the very natural emotions associated with "real life", rendering them inept to handle things like criticisms (be it constructive or otherwise), heartache, rejection, a difference in opinion, or a lack of social contact for extended periods of time without feeling that their relationship is less authentic.

Friendship looks different to different people but is usually built on the basis of common interests, ambitions, mutual respect, ways of life, and a genuine interest in and concern for the well being of one another. There are instances where one individual is the authentic friend, while the other just benefits from the friendship. One may maneuver to ensure that within the realm of their ability, their friend's needs are met while the recipient of those gestures are either unwilling, unable, or feels unrequired to extend those same gestures in return. I have had both reciprocal and non reciprocal friendships, and I've also had friendships that started one way and ended up the other. In these next two stories I'm going to give an example of each. In the first example, I recount my experiences with a family I identify as the first "second family". The reason I refer to them in that way is because since interacting with them I've been blessed to share in and be embraced by many other "second families". In the second example, I detail my experience in an appreciated but non reciprocal friendship. Of course this too is a matter of my own perception being reality. The events timings are very close which makes this all the more interesting.

"The first 'second family' taught me the importance of consistency. For them there wasn't a need to be filled. There wasn't any selfish motive. There was only purity of intent and a willingness to share. The first 'second' family didn't have much more than my family did by way of resources to start. We lived in the same area; in fact, they lived across the street from me, and our families often struggled financially in tandem. Despite this struggle there was always a warm meal for me at their house while sometimes there wasn't one at my own. The language of love and purity of intent was what was communicated quite literally, as the parents in this household didn't speak English well. It was their consistency in presence, consistency in love, and the independence of need (selflessness) that made me evaluate my own family, our values, our consistency, strength, and goodness. That family's consistency made me question whether or not we were doing it right. My household was a young family opposed to the more seasoned, more established parents in that household. That is to say the parents in that household were quite a bit older than my own. The message present in that household was that we sacrifice for you to excel, maximize your potential, and make a way. It was because of this family that I became inspired to become licensed to drive, that I learned to drive standard transmission vehicles (not common!), that I got my passport, that I dared to shine and look 'cool' doing it. They offered me a place of serenity during chaotic times, they included me in all their holiday celebrations, they made me a part of their family! They inspired a desire to learn different languages and communicate with different cultures. They encouraged me to grow, and share, and live. They were there even when they didn't know they were, and that's the best kind of presence; a presence uninterrupted, unshaken, and consistent. The foundation this interaction provided allowed for me to stretch, bend, weep, laugh, grow, understand, and BE…not only for my own family, but for countless others, some of whom you will read about in the pages to come. This family teaches me to this very day that no amount of distance, time, language barrier, financial position, or other deterring variable can outshine pure and unconditional love. We have seen each other at our most vulnerable and most triumphant moments and have shared pride in each others successes. I speak highly of the family as a whole because it was the parents welcoming me into their home that made such an impact, but it's the friendship with their son's that provided the background for these things to come together. These friends have over the years become family and it all goes back to the genuine and mutual exchange that serves as the basis for that friendship."

Jorge and I met as classmates towards the end of elementary school. We clicked on the basis of the expectation our family set around public discipline, family honor, and an innate desire to excel...and excel we did! Throughout elementary school, middle school, and high school, we took nearly every advanced placement and honors course we could find. During those years we grew in our friendship individually and collectively as the trials and tribulations of adolescence pushed and pulled us in different directions. Jose was his older brother and because we were all so close in age we often hung out in the same circles, whether they be friends of mine, Jorge's, or Jose's. When I think about the number of experiences we've shared as a group and how we've been present for each other through the challenges of adolescence and adulthood, I have to comment on the fact that we don't see or hear from each other nearly as much as we did when we were children. We don't spend time on the phone, Jorge doesn't have social media, and Jose barely uses his. By the standard set by today's generation, we should not be friends at all. In spite of this, I know I can pick up the phone at any time, drive hours to their doorstep unannounced, or call in a favor and not question their acceptance or willingness to help out. I know that we can pass several months at a time without speaking to each other and end up in each others presence feeling like no time at all has passed, and laugh at the same things with the same intensity we did when we were children. Yes, these kinds of friendships are good for the soul and the authenticity in relationships like that are becoming increasingly more rare.

This second story involves a relationship in which I feel I was a friend to someone who simply benefited from the friendship. Brian and I met in Middle School at the suggestion of a teacher who noted a similarity in our situations at home. You see, my parents had recently separated and that change had been communicated to some of the school admin. A teacher decided that suggesting a friendship with someone going through a similar situation would ease the adjustment and give me (and him) someone to talk to who could relate to the change. In hindsight, Brian was minimally invested and never had an interest in actually becoming friends. That or he didn't know how to be a friend in the way I was to him. Whatever the case, he didn't object to my being a friend to him and in many instances he used that friendship to his advantage.

The foundation that my friendship with Jorge provided allowed for me to feel confident in making friends outside of his circle. In middle school, although we walked to school every morning together, we had a different set of classes and as a result made different sets of friends. When my teacher suggested I reach out to Brian I thought it a good idea for two reasons;

1. I never thought I'd be in a situation where my parents would split up and wasn't sure how to handle it, and

2. I felt like I had something to offer Brian as we coped with the changes in our circumstances together.

Brian and I spent a lot of time together in the summer months to follow our introduction. Brian, being much less sheltered than I, helped expose me to a lot of the street mentality present within our age group and environment, a stark contrast to the sheltered life I'd lived up to that point. I began to become conscious of what I wore in comparison to others and how I wore it. During this time baggy clothes were what was "in" and nearly no one wore clothes their size. More than that I became conscious of language; the slang terms popular to that time. Accessories, name brands, gadgets, expectations around how to walk, talk and act, and even how to interact with females. I detail this so specifically because up until that point in my life things like name brands, flashy exteriors, and even the pursuit of females weren't things taught or examined in the household. Sure, there was always this concept of "do you have a girlfriend?" present, but Brian exposed me to the pursuit of "the fish". Oh yea, we're talking 1st base, 2nd base, 3rd base, home! He claimed to have achieved sexual contact and I knew none the better but to marvel. This teaching function Brian provided, along with the amount of time spent together was reminiscent of my interaction with Calvin. It was hands on, it was outside of my realm of experience, it was intimate and regardless of our being the same age, seemingly compassionate mentorship. What it really was however, was the beginning of a sort of rites of passage. Most parents, or mentors for that matter, are not going to be attached to the child at all hours of the day and direct their social whereabouts at every turn. However, it was a void I sought to fill that did start as a result of a missed opportunity that made me susceptible to the influence and direction of my peers; Peers who projected to know and experience much, but in reality knew and experienced very little more than I had which is a dangerous and scary concept. Perhaps without the common sense I had and the foundation planted by the many elders and mentors I *did* have growing up, Calvin or Jorge or Brian could have suggested I do something self destructive, or illegal, or harmful to others and I followed through. Is this not a story we see frequently? Young people, males and females, engaging in acts that were thrown down as challenges, dares, suggestions, etc. and completed in the name of "friendship" or street credibility? The 'rites of passage'? Think about your own experience. How many things have you attempted, or started because of the prodding suggestion of a friend? Did you do it for the acceptance? The acknowledgement? What about children now with much less the ability to discern friendship from social media popularity? How many instances of suicide in young children have we heard of as a result of cyber bullying, or rejection, or a relationship gone bad?

Due to Brian's seemingly apparent concern for my well being and social adjustment you can say I felt gratefully devoted to him. If there was anything I could do to help Brian, I would. Brian, being of the same age saw this as a golden opportunity to request of me things that he wouldn't do in return; purchasing things, traveling to and from his home, homework, small incidental things that began to add up. When what was requested of me was denied, I was a "bad friend", I wasn't there for him, we couldn't be friends anymore. The singe of abandonment taunted me and kept me "loyal", even in the face of name calling and verbal abuse. It amused Brian to taunt and tease me then reel me in under the guise of friendship and loyalty. I knew better, but emotionally I wanted that friendship more than it made sense to me.

My efforts didn't go unnoticed though. As a loyal friend seemingly I kept Brian out of trouble. I'll never forget the day his father approached me and shook my hand thanking me for it. "Thank you for keeping my son out of trouble" he said. I couldn't understand back then how or what it was I did, but at that moment I felt like maybe I ended up being the mentor after all. In hindsight, I was the one person Brian spent the majority of his time with. As a result, my influence on him via my own moral compass seemingly was much greater than his influence on me. I also believe his father could see the point I'm trying to illustrate now; that there was a need for compassionate mentorship and that he wasn't available to give it. That period lasted about 2-3 years and the entire duration I thought Brian was mentoring me, but it turns out I mentored him…compassionately and he turned out all the better because of it. Although my first experience with "reverse mentorship", it wouldn't be my last.

"There are points in life where the people you encounter feel so familiar to you…the problem with that familiarity is that you don't know whether that familiar energy interacted with yours at some point previously to your benefit or to your detriment."

The experience I had with Brian prepared me for many similar scenarios in the future. It taught me that the friendship I wanted should be a two-way street. While I can't admit to never falling into a situation where my friendship with someone else wasn't one way, that interaction made me aware of my ability to influence people while being their friend, and if nothing else, made me much more confident on that front.

CALL TO ACTION #2

"Establish consistency in contact with
your mentor/mentee."

Now that you've engaged someone as your mentor or mentee it's time to establish a regular cadence around contact. That is something you can determine independently but understand that the influence of your presence is going to have an effect on the impact of your influence.

Reread that last line.

The influence of your presence is going to have an effect on the impact of your influence. So long as your mentor or mentee knows that you are there expecting of them, they will be reminded of the obligations of their commitment. There are many ways to facilitate this contact and it doesn't have to be the same every time. A phone call, email, text message, or social media posting, are perfectly acceptable to supplement (but not replace) face to face time to catch up, vent, discuss goals, celebrate successes, or even calibrate and provide critiques on deviation from established norms or expectations. Remember it is the acknowledgement of the mentee's total being that makes this interaction a successful one; more than demonstrating a task or giving homework it's the quality in the interaction that will most benefit the parties involved. For the mentor it's the acknowledgement of progress and influence observed in the articulation of accomplished goals, or the expression of otherwise mundane details that reflect the mentor's influence. Whichever side of the table you sit at, establishing consistency in contact is a basic but invaluable and essential part of the interaction.

THE NEED TO LET GO...

This next story was a learning experience that initially haunted me for several years as I thought of myself a failure. You see, after Brian I had started to kind of come into my own. I was more confident that I would never tolerate a one-way friendship again but that I would greet the opportunity to help others with open arms. Ambitious endeavor, but I thought for sure I could handle it.

Thought...

I met Anthony in a high school gym class. He was the object of some taunting and jesting by peers and he acted out because of it by fighting and carrying on. I don't quite remember the situation surrounding our interacting outside of that class but I know there was a lunch period we started to talk and we connected. I was on the high school wrestling team at the time and we were looking for new prospects, so I invited him to work out with some of the guys on a weight training day half expecting he wouldn't show up. Perhaps I recognized in him pieces of me; a desire to be accepted, liked, understood even. He was looking to be acknowledged. I wasn't the most social person at this time in life but I was friendly enough and he eventually started popping up everywhere I was, looking to hang out. Jorge and Jose were still solid friendships, but we had all gotten use to the differences in our schedules, social lives, and independent circles. Things kind of fizzled out with Brian as we attended different high schools and really didn't make the time to stay connected. At this point, I'd made some acquaintances through my classes, had an off and on girlfriend, and my wrestling teammates, but I didn't really spend my down time with anyone in specific anymore.

Things with Anthony seemed normal enough in the beginning. We hung out, talked about girls, and he started learning how to wrestle with the team. We without doubt became very close. He shared more intimate details of his childhood; painful situations and memories, his relationship with his father (who he didn't quite get along with), ambitions, fears, etc. Our friendship came at a time where things were becoming turbulent at home for me as well. My parents were battling in the courts for custody of me and my siblings, I felt this immense pressure as the oldest to hold things together and keep the peace. I felt like I was being stretched between the two parents and felt responsible for shielding my siblings from the ugly that came about as a result of their war. As Anthony and I got deeper into the fragilities of our own situations, I started to notice him become what I thought initially was protective of me. He was ready to fight anyone at the slightest hint of conflict. Shortly after that I realized that it had become a certain possessiveness. I couldn't move or breathe without him being up under me. It started to make me feel uncomfortable. Sure, he meant well, but it was a bit scary and I began to seek out advice on the situation. Surely he was a great friend to me, as great a friend as I was to him. This was nothing like my friendship with Brian, it was most certainly very reciprocal, albeit overbearing at times. However, I started to notice changes in his behavior; a monopolization of my time, violent outburst when he didn't get his way, threats of self harm, etc. For instance, I'd get a ride to school with Jorge and Jose most mornings as school was easily a 30-minute walk from my house. Anthony would wake up early knowing this fact and walk to my house before I would wake up for school. There wasn't room enough for him to get a ride with us so I'd choose to ditch the ride and walk all the way to school with him. He did this for as long as I felt uncomfortable to tell him to stop, and once I did he had a huge temper tantrum about it. Yeah things had begun to spiral out of control and I wanted to be there for him but it was draining me, robbing me of my energy, my time, even my friendships. I felt trapped by duty and obligation to not let down my friend. I was being held emotionally hostage! I'd felt great sympathy for him. His situation at home was poor; his father was verbally and emotionally abusive, and very controlling. Anthony used our friendship as an escape, literally running away from home at times to come to my house whether I was home or not, and waiting hours on end outside if I wasn't. His father threatened to call the police on me multiple times for "kidnapping" his son when in reality his son was running from him. I frequently flashed back to the feelings of abandonment I felt with Calvin and slowly realized that to Anthony, I was Calvin! Eventually however, it became too much for me to deal with and I had to let him know. I had to escape. In my immaturity I told him I didn't want him coming around me anymore because he was crazy. He asked me not to call him crazy but I did, over and over again. He turned to walk away from me and I told him to "keep walking and don't turn back." Cruel I know, but I had enough and our friendship ended shortly after that.

"…For a long time I beat myself up for 'giving up' on or 'abandoning' my friend. There's no doubt in my mind that I was literally the single most significant person in his life. In fact, one day he told his father in front of me that I knew him better than he did; his own flesh and born blood. I believe it was from that moment forward his father resented me. And to this great 'honor' I suppose you can call it, I repaid him with abandonment… at least that's how I viewed it for a very long time. But when you dive into the concepts of self love, self perseveration, emotional health, or whatever you want to call it, it's very clear to me that I wasn't prepared or equipped to take on the responsibility he wanted to give me. Moreover, parts of me were still searching for that in others myself. He became immensely dependent on me…immensely possessive…to the point of outburst and aggression, to the point of threat of self harm, to the point of a self imposed homelessness. And while I can't claim to have never 'needed' someone to the point of a perceived dependence, I've certainly never threatened self harm as a result of not receiving what I so desperately sought after. Now, in no means am I suggesting he was wrong for feeling the way he did. In fact, for him to see that in me at such a young age was a real eye opener to what and how I share and offer to the world around me. It's one of many moments of reinforcement and inspiration in my developing into who I am today. What I'm saying is that at that point I recognized that I didn't believe I had it in me by means of capacity emotionally, mentally, or physically with respect to time and my own selfish goals, to give him the friendship he needed as he wanted it. And so, he sought it elsewhere. Found it, was taken advantage of, and ended up getting into trouble. I spoke to him once or twice before he was sent away never to be heard from by me again and he told me very matter-of-factly that I was responsible. That it was my fault for abandoning him. I carried that with me for a long time… in some ways I still do. What if he still blames me? I made it a point after that to develop so that I didn't 'abandon' anyone again. I learned to over compensate in my mentorship style. That's not to say I regret my decisions, just the way I went about handling it…because often is the case that one needs to recognize when they don't have it in them to give and just let it go… you can't heal someone at the expense of your own health…that defeats the very instinctual law of self-preservation."

So there you have it, back to this need for compassionate mentorship. He searched for it, thought he found it in me, and I didn't have it in me to give. He found it with a group of people who made him feel included, but also took advantage of his desire to be included. He mistook inclusion for acknowledgment. If ever these words should cross his hands and he recognize the story I hope he can forgive my cruelty and understand now why I chose to do what I did. The lesson here however, isn't an apology or a confession of my faults. It's that sometimes, you need to let go. For your sanity, for your health, even for their health. As a mentor, the responsibility can end up being a sacred one, very often it does. You literally hold the thread of someone's life in your hands be it emotionally, scholastically, financially, religiously, professionally, or socially. You very often have the power to make a difference that will be echoed into eternity. And while this may not be the kind of responsibility you sign up for, it's a role that needs filling. As a mentee, your mentor may just not have what you're looking for. It's important to be open and honest about what your expectations are and how they are or aren't being met. These should be established at the onset of the relationship, however needs change and the relationship becomes fluid. Let it be fluid. If your mentorship no longer serves you then it is completely ok for you to find another mentor. In fact, you should over the course of your life have many mentors, some who stay with you long term and some who go on and serve a purpose for a very limited period of time.

CALL TO ACTION #3

Outline your expectations of the mentorship interaction.

As a mentor discuss your desires for contact and interaction. Is your mentee a representation of you? Do you expect strict adherence to a communication schedule? Will you give feedback, take-aways, or calls to action?

As a mentee discuss what exactly you are looking for from your mentor. Do you want to learn a certain skill? Adopt a behavior? Do you want someone to hold you accountable? Someone you can just talk to and vent without judgment?

Both: What would it take to disrupt your mentorship?

-Be clear

-Be specific

-Be open

THE NEED FOR SILENCE...AND THE NEED TO SPEAK

As I cycle through the scenarios surrounding my growth and wisdom in dealing with interpersonal relationships, two stories stand out to me in particular; One that required my silence, and one that required my speech. Both stories occur at different points chronologically but are best delivered together as contrast in action and in delivery. Understand that my own development was at two different points mentally, socially, and emotionally in each of the scenarios.

The need to be silent occurred during my freshman year of college. I was different than I was in high school. I had definitely stepped into a very confident, almost cocky version of myself. Freshman year of college was an eye opening experience. It was the first time I was away from home and my parents influence. I remember my first night on campus thinking "there is no one here to tell me when to go to bed or wake up. I can literally do whatever I want whenever I want." In that time all the parental lessons for self-sustenance kicked in; How to properly wash clothes, what to eat, time management, basic people management, how to carry yourself publically, etc.

Freshman year I met a host of different people with different backgrounds and levels of preparedness. I'll never forget teaching one of my roommates how to use the correct amount of detergent in his laundry or having conversations about hygiene and how a lack of it affects everyone in the room. I remember not having money for books and fancy furniture, and locating the nearest dollar store for essentials. Most rewardingly I remember making new friends from all over. One particular set of friends I became pretty close with and we would spend hours at a time together. There was huge cultural exchange as I went to a predominately "minority" high school that involved walking through metal detectors and riots every one of my four years in attendance while they went to more predominately Caucasian schools with huge sports programs and extra-curricular activities, never having to shuffle through a metal detector worrying about whether or not they'd miss the first bell for class. One day one of my good friends Matt and I were hanging out alone in his room and we started to talk about some of the deeper, non public thoughts in our minds. Matt shared with me the ponderings of not only self harm up to and including suicide, but also of harm to another. In that moment of revelation, I decided two things:

a) I was not going to react and
b) I was not going to betray his confidence in me.

In hindsight, I recognize the delicate position I was in because by reacting I would possibly demonstrate a level of hysteria this friend anticipated thus alienating him from me. By not reacting I could be encouraging the behavior all the same. Many people would likely say that I should have told someone about what I heard. Here is my thought at the time though, (and I am by no means advising anyone on how to handle or ignore circumstances as grave as these but,) how effective would it be for me to take this obvious trust and help my friend come to the conclusion on his own that maybe he needs help? Help outside of, and in addition to the help my friendship could provide? (Sound familiar?)

I'll share with you that it was very effective because Matt and I went to a student services office shortly after that and we both sat with counselors. Did I need someone to talk to? Not really, but I did it to support my friend. Whether or not he shared with the counselor what he shared with me is unknown and insignificant. What's important is that I was silent and supportive. More than that, Matt told me that my silence surprised him. That he expected me to freak out, and I didn't. That he felt better because I didn't react and simply supported. You see, sometimes you have to be silent, to let people come to conclusions on their own. You have to support them in the direction of what's best for them without telling them what's best for them without passing judgment or issuing praise. Sometimes you just have to be there, genuinely there, without motive or incentive. We all need that person, and we all need to be that person. Matt and I are still friends to this day, and he has thanked me for saving his life. Although I don't claim to have saved anyone personally, it was quite literally my first experience with someone I knew personally contemplating suicide. I am happy to have been thought highly enough of that my words and actions discouraged self inflicted harm and perhaps harm to another.

"When Matt first mentioned self harm, I immediately encouraged counsel. He's made me proud in my efforts to help him out. Suicide was something I'd never dealt with before and the concept honestly intimidated me. I was quite blessed to have had success in convincing him out of it. Always conscious of my words and behavior, I unwrapped many of his deepest thoughts and secrets. He walked away a new person today and his last words to me were "thank you". No, THANK YOU for the experience."

This second story is the exact opposite and happened chronologically first. I was in high school, still very much under the watchful eye of my parents. Chronologically this occurred after the whole scenario with Anthony. I had by then tasted certain freedoms, extended curfew, sleeps overs, etc. I started to spread my wings a bit. I was never really popular but I was known well enough for having wrestled and a distinct personality. I had developed expectations and rules for engaging with me and rules I'd adhere to in engaging with others. In some ways looking back, I was the most perfect me. An acquaintance at the time had suffered a great loss and wasn't handling it well at all. He refused to move, to eat, to wash, to attend school. His name was Cristian and although we weren't quite close friends yet, some of his close friends reached out to me and let me know what was going on. His mother, with whom he was very close, passed away. I'm not entirely sure what brought about them reaching out to me, or what they saw in me at the time, but I felt genuinely moved to reach out and help bring Cristian back from the despair and the social quarantine he imposed on himself. I can't say I remember what words I used to initiate conversation, but I was warned not to expect a response. Not only did I get a response, but we hashed it out and I let him talk. I tried my best to console him and not to patronize him with the cliché and emotionless responses most feel obligated to give when they find out about a loss. Cristian told me that I was the first person who didn't say 'oh wow' or something generic. That I basically didn't walk on eggshells about the matter and that I was sincere in my interaction. That sincerity became the foundation for our friendship.

Eventually he got out of bed, bathed, ate, returned to school and reestablished links to his social life. He thanked me, his friends thanked me, and he and I became friends. I helped to reanimate him by speaking with sincerity at the appropriate time. Timing is everything. Both individuals I have shared with you I am in regular contact with all these years later. There is a mutual love and respect shared on the basis of my timing and appropriate actions in that time. I cannot express enough that the timing and success would be ineffective had I not been sincere. When I think about the bond between mentor and mentee, that relationship cannot be successful without sincerity.

CALL TO ACTION #4

- Be Silent
- Speak

1. I challenge you as a mentor/mentee to establish a rule in your interaction that requires one to be actively silent. This active silence means you are fully present in your interaction without the impulse to respond or interject when the other is speaking. Be it venting, debriefing, or advice, this active silence will allow you to best strategize on your next steps, but better than that allow the speaker time to figure out theirs!

2. I challenge you to not leave a session without having one or the other speak. Sometimes all someone needs to hear is that they are heard or understood. Words of understanding or acknowledgement are a powerful tool to motivate, deescalate, inspire, or teach!

LOYALTY WILL FIND ITS PLACE

In an earlier chapter I discussed the learning experience I had with Anthony. He placed his trust and loyalty in me and I didn't deliver so he placed his loyalty elsewhere. That lesson came at a price for him unfortunately that involved him getting incarcerated. It's a lesson I learned with Calvin first hand as well, leaving me with feelings of abandonment. The lesson here is that loyalty responds absent of morality. That is to say, it finds a home with whoever is seemingly most deserving of it. This next story is about my friend Richard.

Richard and I met in high school as well. We were quite the opposite pair. If you took all of the desirable traits in Anthony, Brian, and Calvin and made it into one person that would be Richard. It sounds unreal that the sequence of friendships occurred in a rhythm where each prepared me for the next one. Richard and I clicked during our stint on the wrestling team. He was new in town and instantly became a hit. Guys feared and respected him, girls threw themselves at him, and he was as charming as they come. I think the basis of our friendship was in Richard seeing in me an opportunity to corrupt my 'innocence' and mold me into a mini him, and my seeing in him an opportunity to save him from his self destructive and toxic behaviors. The more time we spent getting to know each other the more I began to trust him. He projected this knowledge of all things I had been sheltered from, picked up where Brian left off exposing me to the ways of the street, but this time while immersing me in it. My parent's war had created a sort of free for all, and with Richard taking me under his wing there was no telling what I'd get into. I enjoyed being the subject of Richard's acknowledgment. I affectionately called him Rich, and under his wing I became untouchable. No one would mess with me because no one wanted to deal with Rich. Females flocked to me and Rich taught me how to speak my desires into existence with them. He exposed me to smoking, drinking, swearing, dancing, partying, fighting and frequent casual sex. I got my ear pierced with him and my first tattoo. I became rebellious, mean even, and everyone took notice. My grades slipped, I stopped going to class, I went from an A honor student to failing 5 classes at one time. Friends would question me about our affiliation and I would tell them to get out of my facc and mind their business. I thought I was this big bad ass and that I was untouchable.

In spite of all of this though, Richard never encouraged me to be this "bad ass". Richard simply exposed me to his everyday life. And while he seemed to enjoy my enjoying this taste of freedom, he never encouraged me to be anyone other than myself. This only pushed me further down the path as I wanted to hang with Richard in his environment all the time. I stayed out of the house for hours on the front steps of Richard's house smoking "Black & Mild" cigars. I learned to trust him totally and with that, loyalty found its place in someone not inherently bad or malicious, but highly influential. In fact, I wrote my college admission essay on him being the most influential person in my young life. There became a point where people just gave up. They knew that saying anything negative about Richard and his lifestyle would further push me away and that I would potentially cut them off. I was devoted to him, I adored him, and my loyalty knew no bounds.

"I guess it also upsets and offends me that some will hint or suggest that he's having a negative influence on me and that his street savvy will ultimately get us both (however more directly aimed at me) into trouble."

My father shared with me years later that this was a scary time for him because he saw me slipping away and didn't want to widen the gap that had existed between us. Richard played a key role in my development as he was my introduction into the "real world" as most people saw it. He completely obliterated the sheltered walls of my upbringing. More than that though, he had won my loyalty. He could steer me in any direction and more often than not I would have followed. He embodied mentorship and the intimacy therein. I became comfortable discussing my fears, my triumphs, insecurities, and doubts. I explained to him every situation prior leading me to value his mentorship; from Calvin to Anthony. It was only later in life, after everyone knew the name Rich and the significance he held that I learned that even blind loyalty knew its limits. That I learned that no one is perfect and I was struck by the very nature I had come to admire, that trust is not a commitment, but an expectation. Choosing to trust someone doesn't guarantee they won't break that trust. It's no insurance against heartache or betrayal, it's simply an expression of "I hope you don't take this vulnerability and use it to my disadvantage and hurt me".

In retrospect, as a mentor it's important to realize how powerful one's influence can be in that state of total surrender. Your responsibility as a mentor is to appropriately wield that influence and understand that as a parent, teacher, guide, uncle, big brother, ect., there is huge potential for a young mind to be led astray on the bases of acknowledgement and trust alone. That your intention may never be to guide a young mind astray, but your actions may.

I learned a lot from Richard's friendship. I grew a lot as well. I learned who I wasn't and that taught me a little bit more about who I was and who I wanted to be. Richard went on to do some things that ultimately betrayed my trust and devastated me. He was a hero in my childhood who turned into a monster in adulthood. It put things into perspective for me and taught me at the end of the day, I needed to be my own hero… and from that day on I was just that.

When childhood hero's become monsters in adulthood

When childhood hero's become monsters in adulthood trust and admiration turn to fear.

Broken bones and bruises yet, have nothing on a broken heart and tears.

And a world once constructed; impenetrable by most, can cave in on itself trapping no one but the host.

Faith in no one, fear and doubt, anger even comes 'round about.

Trust is questionable, love supreme? Makes you wonder if it was all a dream.

Good times, laughs, and memories gone; growin' pains swoon in, a new dawn.

Out with the old, in with the new, reconstruction is on you.

You combat thoughts of failure and defeat.

You wipe your tears; you plant your feet.

You're the hero of this story, you move on to claim your glory.

Questions linger, thoughts remain...happiness will come, embrace the pain. Be unyielding, don't submit. A childhood hero? Doesn't fit.

Learn your lesson, be proud of mistakes; efforts rewarded, an emotional rebate.

Find a mirror, this piece of glass.

Always remember, this too shall pass!

-Rahkim Sabree

CALL TO ACTION #5

Deal breakers!

Create a list of deal breakers for your mentor or mentee. These are "rules" that once articulated, you both know not to break.

Respect and trust for one another are the biggest cornerstones to any relationship. It's important for these boundaries to be established early, and sometimes reminded of often in the initial stages of building the mentorship bond.

THE NEED TO TRAVEL (OUTSIDE OF YOUR COMFORT ZONE)

Originally this chapter was going to be specifically for the mentee. I thought to myself for a second how impactful extending this lesson to the mentor could be on future success. You, the mentor or mentee are in a situation you've never been in before. You don't have the answers and you don't know where to begin to look or ask questions. You have absolutely no direction and have no idea what is expected of you. What do you do?

Imagine traveling across the Atlantic Ocean to a country where the spoken language is not your native tongue. You are traveling alone with no set itinerary but your arrival and departure dates. You are alone in this country for 7 days and you know nothing and no one. Where do you start?

Both scenarios listed above can be challenging why? Because they are unfamiliar and uncomfortable! And while different people would have different answers for the set of scenarios outlined above, one thing rings true and that is that both situations lie outside of the comfort zone, and it is in that very spot that the most growth occurs! Traveling outside of your comfort zone both literally and figuratively is a needed experience. You learn new things about the world, about others, and most importantly about yourself.

"To date I've been to six countries, two of them twice, and I've traveled to several states domestically in the USA. By no means of the imagination do I consider myself "well traveled" as I have several friends who have seen much more of the world than I, but what I'm saying is that for at least 6 times I've chosen to leave my home country, the customs therein, my family, a currency system I'm use to, occasionally foods I'm use to, and most recently the language I speak and am use to, to venture off into the unknown. Now, whether that be for education, a special occasion or event, the experience, or a combination of the mentioned, each time I return home with a little more appreciation for small comforts and luxuries, as well as the knowledge of how other customs, languages, etc play a role in the daily interactions of people who have seen more than their own 'backyard'. To travel is a requirement to me because it breaks down walls of isolation...be they self imposed or societal. I've faced many fears, realized the mythology in some depictions of interactions with certain peoples, and have created my own ideas about the circumstances, peoples, and cultures I've been involved with."

My grandfather use to say to me that the best means of education are traveling and reading. That is traveling first, and reading second. I've held on to that and will live out his teaching while teaching others that there is absolutely no substitute to travel. I say that with great confidence because traveling can occur more than just physically. Sure you can get on a boat, a plane, a train and travel to an unfamiliar destination; but you can also travel by situation or circumstance, by exposure to depths or boundaries in thought or by feeling, not previously experienced.

As a mentor being a guide in that unfamiliar terrain (be it figuratively or literally) will build credibility and trust in you by your mentee. You will have to be intuitive, alert, and aware of just how far to allow your mentee to venture out and just how much your mentee can handle. As a mentee, trusting in your mentor and using them as support can broaden your horizons, your experiences, and even possibly your skill sets as you may learn something and go on to express that learning on a continuous basis. Many people shy away from experiencing the unfamiliar because they are afraid to fail. With the right mentor in place you will learn that failure is a part of learning! That with that support and reassurance in place, there is no such thing as failure because they are going to see it coming before you do. I have a mentee, Jason who I took on his first trip cross country. It was the first time he'd been on a plane. To describe the amount of growth I noted in him in less than 5 days just by being able to spread his wings would be a disservice to the extent of the influence that trip had on him. I literally watched as he stepped into a different kind of confidence, aspiration, and determination to be and do more. I also watched that seed grow over time into a hunger for other trips to other places with or without me. That was truly a satisfying moment for me as a mentor to say look at the fruit of the seeds I've planted.

Let's take a step back however because as a mentor or a mentee that's not all you'll ever be is it? It's not what defines you as a person. It's important in fulfilling either of these roles to also remember that you are indeed a person; your own person. In remembering that, I would encourage you to take this chapter's suggestion of 'the need to travel' simply to get away and decompress. Sometimes we have to step out of the role to figure out or ground in who we are as an individual. The scenario I opened with, being in a foreign country for 7 days alone knowing nothing and no one was not hypothetical; At least not for me it wasn't.

I traveled alone to my dream city of Barcelona, Spain. Those 7 days tested me in ways I'd not previously been tested; mentally, spiritually, and even physically. I had no cheat code, no guide, just intuition and a blank canvas of imagination. I fell in love on that trip however. I fell in love with the land, the culture, and most of all I fell in love with me.

"I'm literally sitting in the grass in a foreign country under the sun just taking it all in. It's liberating to think that at this very moment not a soul knows who I am, what I'm capable of, what languages I do or don't speak, whether or not I'm educated, etc. All anyone knows is that I exist... I doubt highly that if I were back home I'd be laying in anyone's public grass but my own."

"The truth is I'm terrified...I've been terrified the entire time...before even boarding my first flight. I'm excited and learning and moving forward but I am afraid! But fear is an illusion and a natural reaction to the unknown. Tomorrow if I venture into the same area I went into today I will feel more confident since I've been there. It is my greatest belief now that fearlessness is an illusion...like fear, it's projected [outward] rather than internal to demonstrate to others that you are not afraid... but you are, you just choose to move forward. The difference between fearlessness and bravery is a matter of internal motivation to keep going!"

"Barcelona has been nothing short of awe inspiring. Rich in history and architecture. Although the inspiration itself comes from my journeying here alone, the sights to take in have awakened in me a solace, a peace, an understanding not often felt or experienced. It's inspired me to want to disconnect. To wander into places unfamiliar to me and just be with me... yes Barcelona has forced me to be alone with me...and although I'm often alone physically, I'm not always spending time with me. Here, no one knows me, judges me, or thinks anything about me... and if they do it wouldn't matter. Out here I'm invisible. I can disappear without a trace or anyone batting an eye or raising an eyebrow... and that is simultaneously invigorating and terrifying. My first leg of this trip is nearing its end and I've learned so much... am grateful for so much... I've learned to be brave, be patient, be decisive, slow down, be in the moment, disconnect, reconnect, appreciate, share, explore, be confident, that I'm never really alone. I've learned to rely more on my ancestors... I've learned I have to do more and be more for me. That everything I need is already inside of me waiting to come out, BEGGING to come out. That time is an illusion...that we are all existing all the time, at the same time. This trip has made me question, when did I stop loving myself first? The most? And why? Who is more deserving of my love than I? NO ONE!"

One more lesson about leaving your comfort zone I actually learned from Jason in reverse mentorship. Sure, I've mentored a mentor before, but it's been the learning experience in mentoring Jason that has taught me about acknowledgment, patience, breaking down walls, earning trust, and accountability as a mentor.

Previously, as a mentee I've been able to record my experiences, my desires and needs, my list of "will and won't do's" … but it's been through Jason I've learned by trial and error that a mentor and mentee may have different ideas about mentorship and the direction it grows. That the seeds that you plant may bare fruit that doesn't grow upright, but vines along in a different direction. That you may want more for your mentee than they want for themselves, and that most importantly, your job is to guide not command. Jason didn't have the words initially to tell me his wants and needs as a mentee. It was again, trial and error based on my own reflection and recollection of what I wanted out of a mentor. Mentorship is in many ways a partnership that can be terminated at anytime by any party. As a mentor it's important to check your ego and let your mentee grow (albeit guided) in the direction they want to grow. If we go back to the lesson of "loyalty" found with Rich, he NEVER forced me to accept his lifestyle. He was him, and he let me be me… ENCOURAGED me to be me. It was the authenticity in our interaction that made me want to adopt his lifestyle, or at least submerge myself in it.

When I accepted Jason as a mentee, I tried to shape and mold him. He quickly grew tired of feeling like he couldn't be himself around me. He respected me, trusted me, even wanted to make me proud, but he shared with me that he felt conflicted; like he had to be a certain way around me. I could feel the strain on our relationship grow as I tried to make him successful by merit of ritual and the structure I thought he needed or "worked". My proudest moment with Jason is when he came to me and told me that this wasn't working. That he needed to feel like he could breath and be himself around me; that I needed to check my ego. I checked my ego and our relationship flourished… of all I've been able to accomplish with him, I felt that was the greatest because I had groomed my mentee to mentor me! He had to travel outside of his comfort zone and I had to do the same. It's often easy as a mentor to forget that you too are human and prone to error. That you do not have all the answers, and that a lot of the time you are probably just figuring it out as you go along.

CALL TO ACTION #6

1. Foster an environment where reverse mentorship can occur. You as the mentor will NOT have all the answers all the time, AND THAT'S OK! Your mentee should feel comfortable giving you an evaluation of your mentorship in the same way they would expect you to give them an evaluation of their development. I make it a point to be open to learning from anyone and everyone.

2. Travel outside of your comfort zone! That includes literal travel and figurative travel. You can take an adventure through books and movies, try a new food, visit that weird new exhibit, listen to the hot new song all the kids love, take a road trip, ANYTHING! Learn to get comfortable being uncomfortable and share that discomfort as you navigate it together or alone. Document your experiences and share as a learning example.

LOVE YOURSELF, HEAL YOURSELF, KNOW YOURSELF (BARCELONA)

In the last chapter I focused not only on stepping outside of your comfort zone, but also stepping outside of your role as mentor and mentee. This is necessary due to the fact that very often in these relationships we absorb or take on responsibilities not inherently our own but accept it as such. For example, as a mentee you might start to seek and depend on your mentor's approval. This can be dangerous depending on the mentor's intent, but also because you might lose your sense of direction when it comes to your own goals or ideas about how to accomplish them. You might start trying to anticipate what makes your mentor happy when the reality is that what makes your mentor happy is very likely you realizing YOUR goals and aspirations.

On the flip side as a mentor you might take responsibility for some heavier issues impacting your mentee. Perhaps there are road blocks that fall outside your sphere of influence. Perhaps your mentee is dealing with depression or thoughts of self harm. Perhaps your mentee is caught up in some financial or domestic struggles. Naturally, as a guide you will want to help. Subconsciously or even consciously you might begin to view your mentee through the vein of his struggle and take on the obligation to 'be there' for him not realizing you're overcompensating. The nature of how involved or uninvolved you as a mentor want to be is entirely up to you however, in building these relationships and understanding that a need exist you will likely take a position of action rather than inaction. In both scenarios you lose a piece of yourself, and if you aren't careful you'll continue to lose pieces until you can't recognize yourself anymore.

With that, you need to understand both as a mentor and mentee that you need to know your limitations and know how to recharge. "Love yourself, heal yourself, know yourself" means in simplest terms that you need to value yourself first, take action around recharging, and know what you are qualified to take on by way of capacity or expertise. This was the lesson of my interaction with Anthony earlier on and a lesson I'd be reminded of during my trip to Barcelona. In both instances I needed to let go, disconnect, and come back reconnected. In order to love yourself you have to know yourself. In order to heal yourself you need to recognize the love you have for yourself.

For as long as I can remember I've been fulfilling duties akin to mentorship to others. I frequently thought of myself as having to 'have it all together' or 'be strong for' (insert person name here). It wasn't until I realized that I was silently battling with depression that I was literally forced to understand this principal of "Love yourself, heal yourself, know yourself'. Literally months had gone by before I realized there was an issue. I started eating more, gaining weight, and ceasing exercise. I remember looking at myself in the mirror and feeling disgusted and angry but not having any desire to do anything about it. I remember wanting to stay in bed all day and not move. I remember getting half dressed to go hang out with friends and then deciding at the last minute that I didn't want to go anymore and turn off my phone. I stopped doing things that I loved to do to do nothing in its place. In spite of all of this, I still didn't see the signs. I woke up and I smiled in everyone's face pretending that I was fine because at the moment I felt 'ok'. That is until one day everything was going wrong and I had gotten in my car to head home and I was frozen in my seat. I remember telling myself repeatedly to turn the car on and drive, asking myself why I'm just sitting here. I remember feeling a feeling I had never felt before and I just started calling everyone in my phone. When no one answered or could stop doing what they were doing I started on the road home and just broke down. I cried the whole way home, sat in the parking lot and cried, and then got in the house and cried some more. I never felt more defeated and confused. I was angry with myself for crying and not knowing why. I didn't know what was happening to me but I knew it wasn't good.

Literally nothing triggered my tears but the fact that the day was a little crappy and yet I was crying. It was then that I started to put 2 and 2 together. It was then that I realized I was dealing with symptoms of depression. That wouldn't be the last episode I'd have either. As time progressed I'd develop anxiety attacks as well.

"...I sat at the edge of my mom's bed and began to tell her of the horrible feelings and thoughts I had. How my mind tried to convince me I was worthless, undeserving of love, lazy, and a slob, among other things. That I was ugly and fat. That I'd just get fatter and uglier. As I described it to her my eyes filled with tears and I got upset because I began to cry and I didn't know why... nor did I have the control to stop it. I reflect to the few people I've told about it and the varied responses from "what do you have to be depressed about?" to "It's all in your head." to "what can I do to help?" In hindsight that was a very building time for me but scary as well. I didn't feel like "me" ... I felt like there was someone else inside my head making me crazy!"

That feeling of 'crazy' is what upset me the most in dealing with anxiety and depression. That feeling of "I thought I knew who I was and this is definitely not me but it is me" is frightening. I had to take steps to remedy this and fast! I used a 3 prong approach to self healing. I decided to root myself in the spiritual, work on building up my mental, and to develop in some capacity physically. I also sought counseling. I started practicing Kung Fu to help bridge the spiritual, mental, and physical while focusing in the now. In being completely present. Dealing with those types of conditions are never just one and done. It's a continuous effort for me to stay on top of my mental and emotional health. I share this with my mentor(s) and mentee(s) for a couple of reasons namely accountability (you know that if I'm going through something and withdraw that I'm not just ignoring you or that I'm not upset with you) and support (I know that if I'm having an episode that I can contact you and feel like you will offer support in my moments of weakness). In spite of all the understanding, the check in's, the encouragement, the reassurance, the space and advice, fulfilling the need for me to travel outside of my comfort zone, as mentioned in the previous chapter, has been my saving grace. It was in Barcelona that I began to write the words that fill these very pages. Learning who I am, loving myself, and initiating healing prevented me from sinking into the abyss of my own mind.

CALL TO ACTION #7

Mental Health checks!!

It's as important as a mentor to do mental health checks as you do "pulse checks" on the work and development your mentee does.

It's important as a mentee to be open to sharing the truth about how and why you feel "bad". Too many men (young and older) suffer in silence. The purpose of a mentor is to be your sounding board and your strength. We've already established that the mentor isn't always going to have all the answers. However, the mentor is present to guide and acknowledge... and that acknowledgement is free. Make mental health checks a regular part of your conversation.

"PAY IT FORWARD"

As a mentor you will likely derive great joy from seeing your mentee succeed. Success is a very subjective term when you take a look at it, so to be specific success to me is that my mentee accomplishes what he established as a goal. Sure, I have my own ideas about what I'd like to see him accomplish and as a mentor I should be challenging him to experience and desire to accomplish more. However, one of the biggest lessons (and growing pains) I've experienced as a mentor is that your mentee is there for your guidance and suggestion, not for you to dictate to and control. I began to introduce this in the chapter about traveling outside of your comfort zone where I introduce Jason. However, I want to fill you in on the details around how Jason became more than a mentee, and more like a brother. To elaborate, Jason and I established our mentoring at transitional times in both our lives. I had just experienced a major relocation which was life changing, He was on the brink of breakdown and confused about where to turn and what to do. He was slow to trust, and hard to convince of my commitment to his development and success. In fact, we've spent many cumulative hours where I've tried to make him understand that as being my intention to prove I was here to stay. Jason and I, while building out our mentorship also built out a friendship. The trust I eventually gained from him as someone who would guide and advocate for his success with his best interests at heart, (both by demonstration and articulated experiences) would serve as one base layer, while the relaxed and relatable nature of our friendship served as another. This allowed for us to forge a bond akin to brotherhood. For me as the mentor this was a balance that was not easy to strike as the success or failure in one role could (and often did) impact the other. There were many instances where as a mentor I would have a very strong position against what I as a friend would have been expected to be ok with (and vice versa). Over time I started to watch him adopt my influence and guidance, and morph in his thought forms and even his interests. He soon began to realize he had so much potential and influence, but not without others noticing first.

Jason is one of those people who naturally draws other people to him. He has the ability to change the moods of others just by being in a mood himself. I committed to Jason my mentorship and I told him in return, he has to go out and be for someone what I am to him. That he needs to pay it forward. As Jason grew in knowledge and experiences around a variety of different things, others began to take notice and started tapping him on the shoulder for support. I had to be very careful to arm Jason against this particular type of predator as they come in the guise of someone needing your 'help'. Thankfully, Jason was able to mostly navigate these people who wanted to use and take advantage of him while continuing to consciously influence to encourage and help grow others.

Besides having to learn to *influence him and not control him* I've also had to learn to:

- let him make mistakes
- let him take the lead on learning activities/engagement
- hold him accountable for his actions/inactions
- remain consistent
- ALWAYS do what I say I'm going to do.

Of all the things I learned, Jason has let me know that the thing that stood out in separating me from other mentors he's had is that anything I've ever committed to him I've made happen. I met him more than half way many times and in doing so taught him how to meet me half way back.

This is important for both the mentor and mentee to take note of because that is the foundation on which you build to make each other better. You have to reach towards each other by setting expectations, boundaries, and commitments around follow up and delivery with respect to the structure you create.

Jason and I not only discuss the spectrum of issues, concerns, roadblocks, fears, accomplishments, etc relating to him, but also the 'why' behind my position, approach, and decisions in guiding him. I share this with him because he now understands my intent when I make a decision and, when he delivers on his commitment to pay it forward he'll have a baseline of strategies and approaches to handling his own mentee and their unique set of challenges he'll be faced with. Paying it forward is so important in our environment as we quickly forget that we were once in the very shoes of the people we mentor. Individually I'm certain that most of us has experienced that lost confusion and wished that we had someone to help guide us through it. We owe it to ourselves to provide that for someone else.

CALL TO ACTION #8

Pay it forward!

Teach your mentee how to be the best mentor they can by being the best mentor you can be. Create an expectation (as a mentor) that your mentee will mentor others in the future.

Commit (as a mentee) to "paying it forward" and mentoring someone who needs mentoring in the way you were mentored.

MY MENTOR

"My consistency will break your inconsistency"

I met one of my most involved mentors' freshman year of high school when I joined the wrestling team. Coach Al and I started off at odds. He had a very aggressive almost abrasive personality and he made a habit of giving the new guys nick names. I happened to be wearing a black shirt to practice the day he decided to nickname me 'black shirt'. I'd been familiar with hazing practices in any organization but, *"I had developed expectations and rules for engaging with me and rules I'd adhere to in engaging with others"*. At the end of practice, I approached Coach Al and asked him how he'd like me to refer to him and he replied "Coach". I extended my hand and told him my own name. He looked around the room and laughed with the more senior teammates and he said to me, "Son, no one here gets called by their name." From that day forward however, he called me by my name. Coach has been present for nearly every adventure I'd encountered from the time we met onward. He helped me deal with my parent's custody battle, he advised me on the matters that span nearly every scenario and relationship I've articulated in these pages, and he encouraged me to be me always.

As our bond grew, my trust in him grew so much so that even years after leaving the high school wrestling team I referred to him as Coach and modeled my own mentorship practices after our encounters. Coach is responsible for coining the phrase "My consistency will break your inconsistency." And it's that lesson in consistency that has carried me through the many mentor/mentee scenarios I've been apart of. It's that lesson in consistency that has kept me on the right side of trouble, focused in my endeavors, present in my relationships, and sincere in my approach. It is his mentorship that has taught me what it is about me that draws people to me, that makes me so special, so influential, so unique. What was his secret? He let me be me. He guided, praised, encouraged positive choices, discouraged negative choices, was compassionate, and sincere in his dealings with me. And he always let me be me.

"Without looking directly for a 'father figure' I did want an older male to treat me with respect, to care, to love, to role model. Someone I could learn from and look up to…"

Coach Al was all of those things. He once told me that he'd be whoever and whatever I needed him to be. That I made the relationship. As he watched me grow from adolescent to adult, he's never not been there for me to call, at any hour, or any day. He's seen the full spectrum of my emotions, heard the depth of my fears, celebrated in my successes, and no matter what has always told me he was proud.

There is no call to action for this chapter as we've reached the end of this work. Just a reminder of the lasting and powerful influence you will have as a mentor on the life of boys to men. Anyone can be a mentor, and frequently everyone is whether by accident or in a deliberate and formalized fashion. Be conscious of the need that exists in boys and young men. YOU define what it means to be a man or a brother. Know who can slip in and under your influence. Internalize the lessons present with Rich and loyalty, with Calvin and abandonment, with Jason and checking your ego… It won't always be easy; in fact there will be some really trying days and trying personalities.

It WILL however, always be worth it.

ABOUT THE AUTHOR

Rahkim Sabree grew up in the small inner city neighborhood of Mount Vernon, NY. He is passionate about Mentorship mechanics in young men and Financial Literacy education. Rahkim is available to speak on both topics and is eager to share how his story has shaped him, his perspective, and his approach to education and mentorship.

www.ingramcontent.com/pod-product-compliance
Lightning Source LLC
Chambersburg PA
CBHW071340290326
41933CB00040B/1848